Your Body
Treasures Inside

by Donna Koren Wells
illustrated by Helen Endres

Created by

Distributed by CHILDRENS PRESS®
Chicago, Illinois

Grateful appreciation is expressed to Elizabeth Hammerman, Ed. D., Science Education Specialist, for her services as consultant.

Library of Congress Cataloging in Publication Data

Wells, Donna K.
    Your body ; treasures inside / by Donna K. Wells ; illustrated by Helen Endres ; created by Child's World.
        p. cm. — (Discovery world)
    Summary: A simple introduction to the various parts of the human body and their functions.
    ISBN 0-89565-576-4
    1. Human Anatomy—Juvenile literature.   [1. Body, Human.]
I. Endres, Helen, ill.   II. Child's World (Firm)   III. Title.
IV. Series.
QM27.W45   1990
612—dc20   90-30632
                                                                CIP
                                                                 AC

1 2 3 4 5 6 7 8 9 10 11 12 R 99 98 97 96 95 94 93 92 91 90

Your Body
Treasures Inside

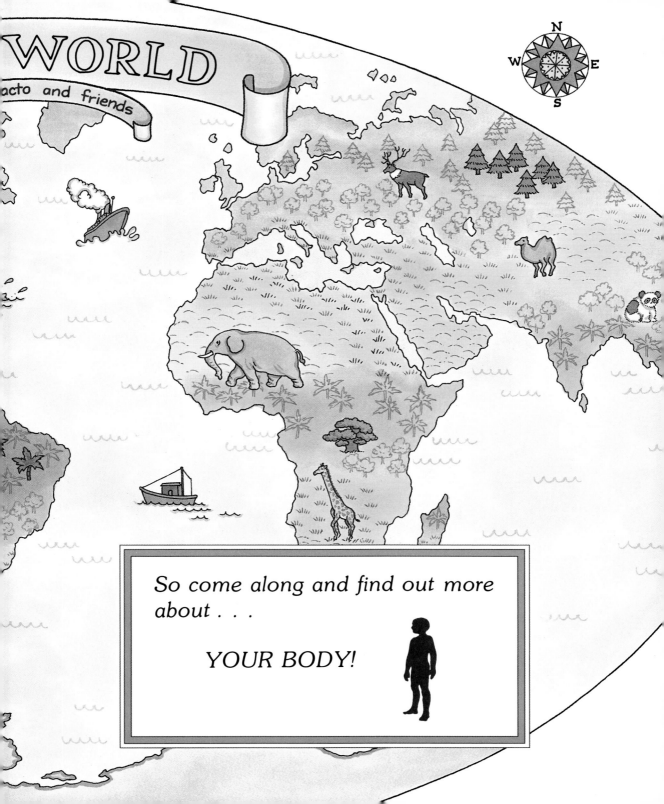

Have you ever thought about what is inside your body? You have many treasures there. You can't see them, but they are very important.

Would you like to know what they look like? Let's go on a treasure hunt and see what we can find.

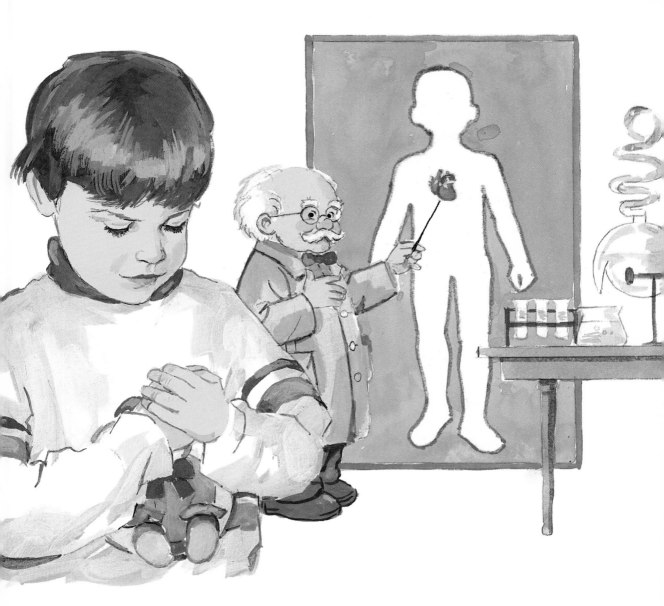

Here's a very special treasure—your heart!
It is close to the center of your chest. If
you put your hand on your chest after you
have been running, you can feel your
heart beating.

Your heart is only about the size of your fist, but it has a very big job. It works as a pump, pushing blood to every part of your body, even to the tips of your toes.

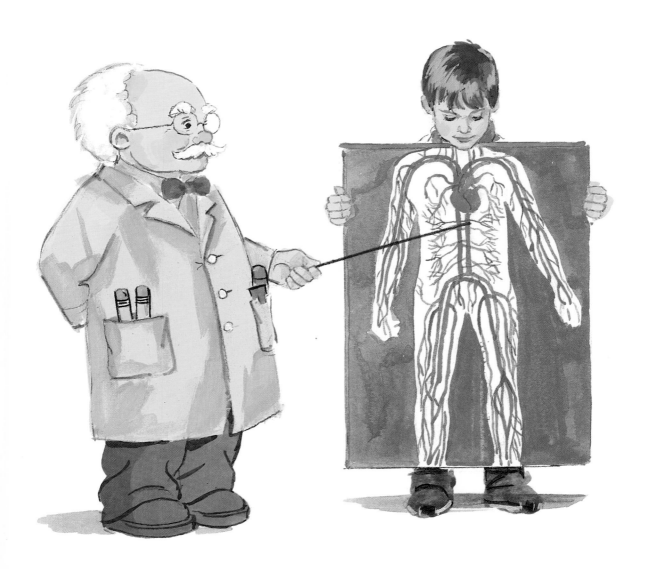

Your blood is pushed through special tubes
called blood vessels. You have many
blood vessels.

Blood is very important. It carries food and oxygen to every part of your body. Your blood is made up of red and white parts called cells.

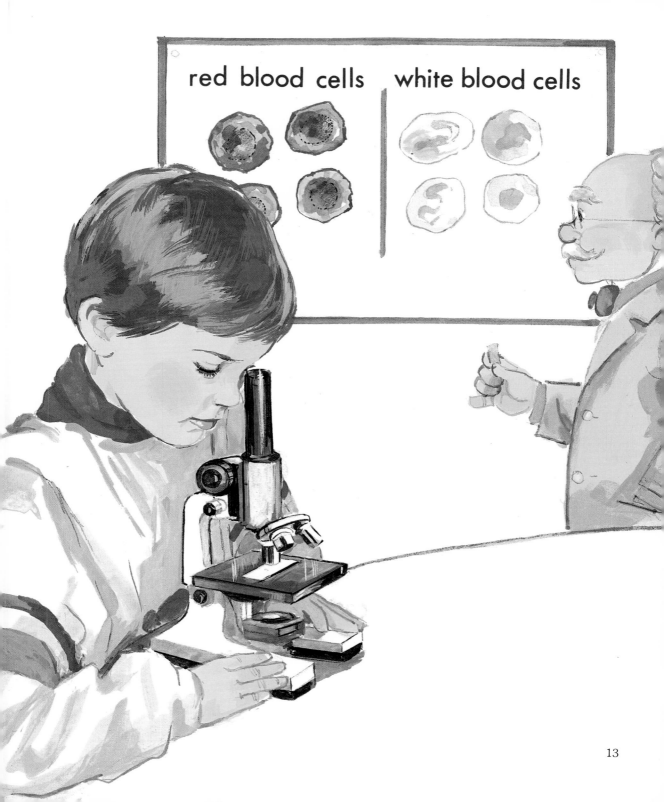

red blood cells　　white blood cells

13

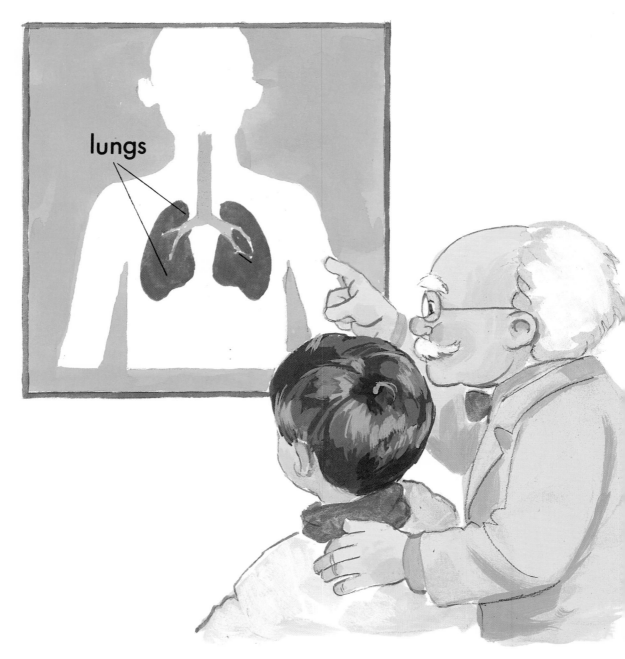

lungs

Do you know where your blood gets the
oxygen it needs? It comes from your lungs.
They take in air. Oxygen is in the air.

Your lungs work like balloons. When you
fill a balloon with air, it gets bigger. When
you fill your lungs with air, they get bigger
too.

Take a deep breath. See how your chest gets bigger? Your lungs are taking in oxygen. Your blood picks up the oxygen and takes it to the rest of your body.

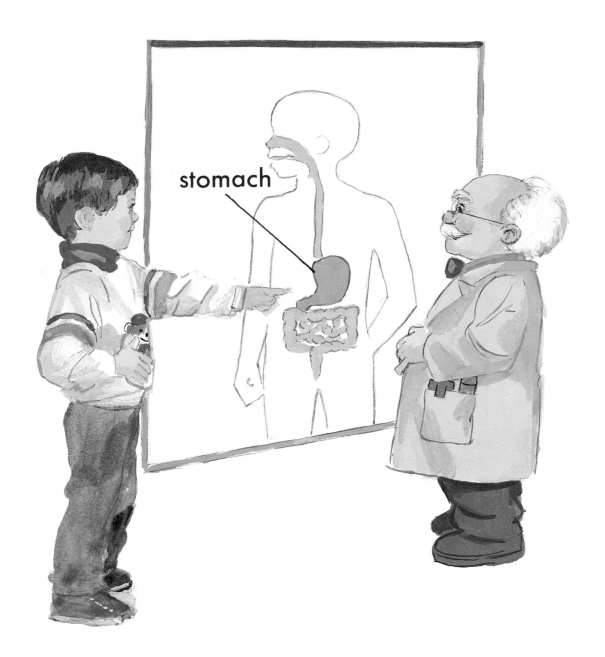

stomach

Right below your lungs is another treasure
—your stomach. When you eat, the food
goes down a long tube into your stomach.

Your stomach is like a blender. It takes all
the food you eat and mashes it up. It gets
the food ready for your body to use.

One way your body uses that food is to keep your bones strong and healthy. If your bones weren't strong, they couldn't hold you up. You would be like a rag doll.

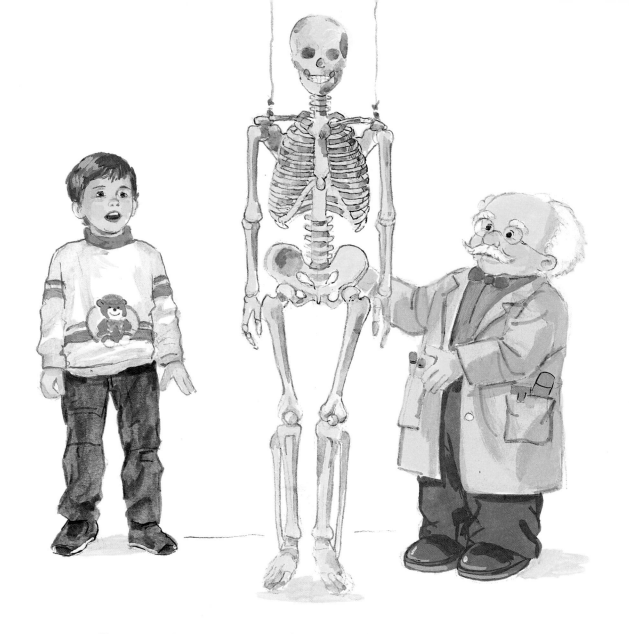

All your bones together make up your skeleton. Your skeleton holds you up and protects all the other treasures inside your body.

But your bones can't move by themselves. That's where your muscles come in. Your bones have muscles attached to them. The muscles pull your bones to make them move.

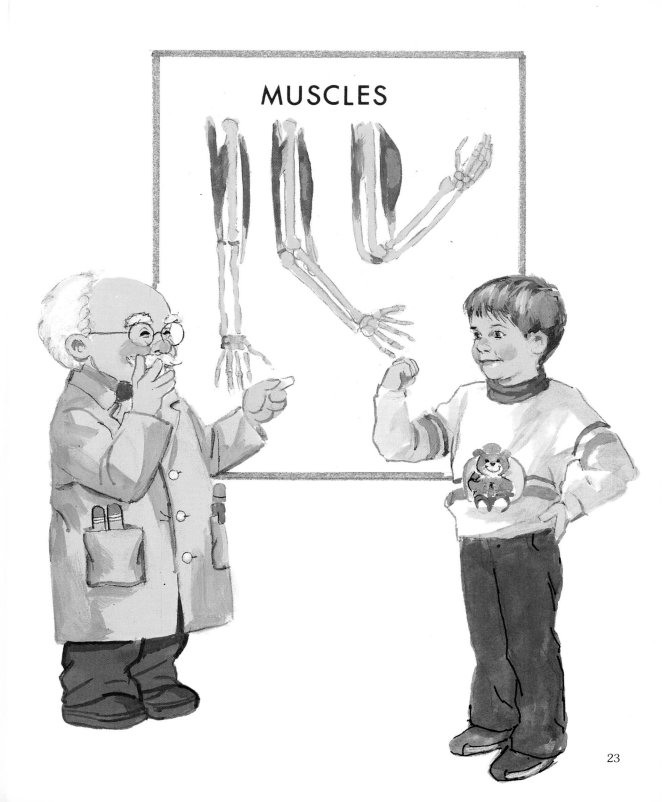

MUSCLES

23

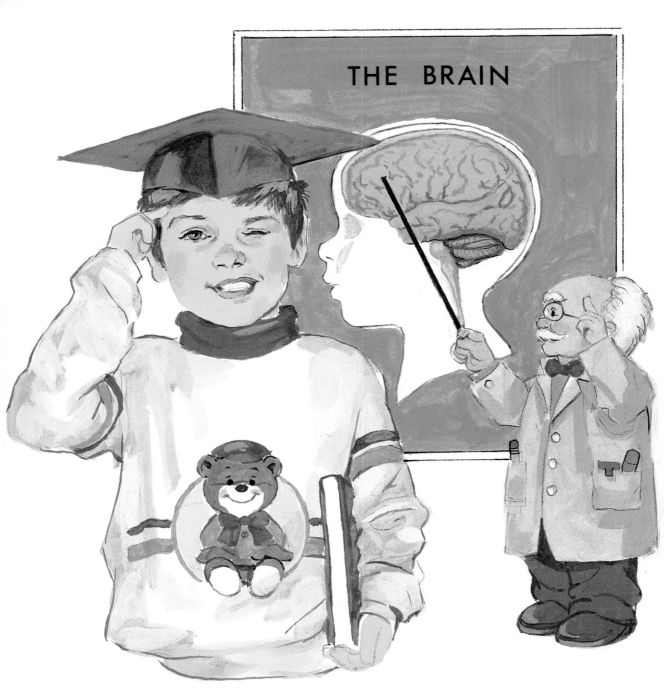

Now we have come to the greatest inside treasure of all—your brain!

Your brain is like a computer. It controls
everything you do.

Through your eyes, ears, nose, mouth,
and skin, your brain takes in messages
from outside your body. If you get too
close to something hot, your skin sends a
signal to your brain.

Then your brain sends a message to your muscles telling them to move away from the hot spot. YOW!

You do your thinking with your brain. And your brain stores information you want to remember. How many inside treasures can your brain remember right now?

MORE TO EXPLORE!

Professor Facto says . . .

You can make a treasure map of your own body! You will need a large piece of paper. (Butcher paper is good.)

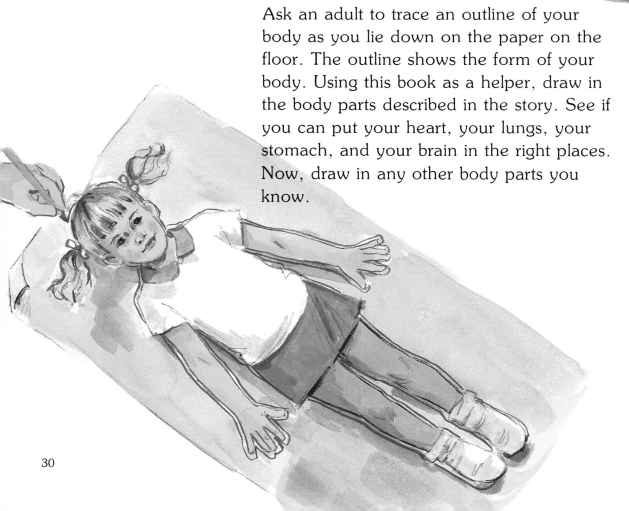

Ask an adult to trace an outline of your body as you lie down on the paper on the floor. The outline shows the form of your body. Using this book as a helper, draw in the body parts described in the story. See if you can put your heart, your lungs, your stomach, and your brain in the right places. Now, draw in any other body parts you know.

Muscle Madness

How do your muscles feel when they are working? Let your right arm hang relaxed at your side. With your left hand, feel the inside of your upper arm. That is where your *bicep* muscle is. How does it feel when your right arm is relaxed? Now make a fist with your right hand, and bend your elbow. How does your muscle change? Find other muscles on your body. How do they feel when you use them?

Stomach Sounds

The stomach is a busy body part. It has to work hard to break down a double cheeseburger! Shortly after a friend has eaten, put your ear to his stomach and listen. (Make sure you have his permission first!) What do you hear?

31

INDEX